The Great Battlefield

The Middle East, whose troubles defined so much of the 20th century, was a g.... . . Britain, in particular, it was the vital route to its most precious imperial possession, India.

When the French historian Ernst Renan welcomed the builder of Egypt's Suez canal, Ferdinand de Lesseps, to the French Academy in April 1885 he quoted the controversial words of Jesus: "I come not to bring peace, but a sword".

"This saying must frequently have crossed your mind," Renan told de Lesseps. "Now that you have cut through it, the isthmus has become a defile, that is to say, a battlefield.

"The Bosphorus by itself has been enough to keep the whole civilised world embarrassed up to the present, but now you have created a second and much more serious embarrassment.

"Not merely does the Canal connect two inland seas, but it serves as a communicating passage to all the

The British failed to join de Lesseps's syndicate to finance the Suez Canal, but soon realised its importance. Disraeli borrowed £4 million personally to buy the shares owned by a bankrupt Egyptian government.

Imperial highway

"They want the Empire to be maintained, to be strengthened; they will not be alarmed even it be increased. Because they think we are obtaining a great hold and interest in this important portion of Africa -- because they believe that it secures to us a highway to our Indian Empire and our other dependencies, the people of England have from the first recognized the propriety and the wisdom of the step which we shall sanction tonight."

From a speech in February 1876 by Benjamin Disraeli to the House of Commons, justifying the purchase of a controlling interest in the shares of the Suez Canal Company.

oceans of the globe. In case of a maritime war, it will be of supreme importance, and everyone will be striving at top speed to occupy it. You have thus marked out a great battlefield for the future."

These prophetic words weigh heavily in a region that has become a source of global instability, marked by a century of war, revolutions and dictatorships. Even so, Renan could not have foreseen the full scale of what was to come. The battlefield soon spread to encompass a region stretching from the Atlantic to the Persian Gulf. It became the centre of a clash of economic giants, world powers, local nationalism, and a conflict between east and west, Islam and Christianity.

Even before the era of oil, the region was a vital bridge between the east and the west. The Suez Canal shortened the route from Europe to the east. Through it passed products vital to Britain: jute, tea, rubber, hemp for ropes, cotton, silk, raw materials and, in due course, oil from Persia and Mesopotamia.

The region was a vital hub for land, rail and air routes. As early as the 1880s Germany planned to construct a railway which would connect its capital with the Persian Gulf – the Berlin-Baghdad railway. That scheme vanished with Germany's defeat in the First World war. Instead, Britain built the Cape-Cairo line, linking its colonies in Africa with a network of railways in the near east, to Cairo, Haifa, Istanbul, Baghdad, Damascus and the holy cities, an "iron hoop" that served to bind together much of the British Empire.

With the rise of air travel, control of bases in the Middle East became vital. The route from London to Bombay, Singapore, Hong Kong and Australia passed through Haifa. The route connecting British East Africa to Cape Town started in Cairo. The French air route to Vietnam and the far east linked Marseilles to Beirut, Baghdad to Bombay.

A foothold in the region would also guarantee access to oil, what George Kennan of the US state department described as "the greatest material prize in world history". At the turn of the 20th century oil had been discovered in Persia (now Iran) and Mesopotamia (now Iraq). In the 1930s what turned out to be the largest oilfield in the world was discovered in Saudi Arabia.

On the eve of the First World War, the Middle East was still ruled by the Ottomans, but by 1917 their Empire had collapsed, and the struggle for the Middle East began. Three forces were involved: America and the imperial powers, local rulers, and the great mass of ordinary people.

The Failure of American Diplomacy

After the collapse of the Ottoman Empire, Britain and France carved up the Middle East between themselves and, fatally, resorted to double-dealing with the Arabs and the Jews over Palestine.

On 20 March 1919, when the major powers gathered for the Versailles peace conference, the US president Woodrow Wilson proposed that an international commission be sent to the Middle East, to gather the views of the peoples of the region ahead of plans to establish a series of Mandates[1].

The US was concerned that the post-war carve-up contained in the Sykes-Picot[2] agreement would result in expanded French and British empires, subsuming the interests of peoples only recently liberated from Ottoman rule. Wilson believed that the indigenous populations should be given independence under the benevolent trusteeship of the major powers, with democratic republics eventually replacing the monarchies and colonial rule. Above all he wanted to dismantle the trade barriers then operated by the major empires, and to open up the world to free trade.

The post-war partition of the Ottoman Empire was driven by competition over the oil fields of Mesopotamia and the Persian Gulf. France wanted to split geographic Syria into five states along ethnic and religious lines, but during the war, in order to win Arab support, the British had already promised the Arab leader, Sharif Hussein, that Britain would support a unified Arab kingdom in Greater Syria, which included not just modern Syria but also Palestine, Lebanon, and much of what is now Iraq.

Arab support alone was not enough to win the war; Britain also wanted to win over the sceptical, anti-colonialist Americans, who had so far remained neutral. Lord Balfour, Britain's foreign secretary, therefore targeted the powerful American Jewish lobby. In 1917, in his famous letter to Lord Rothschild[3], head of the British Jews, he declared that Britain would favour the establishment of a Jewish "national home" in Palestine.

Wilson's international commission was opposed by most other nations. He persisted, and a reduced all-American version, the King-Crane Commission[4], eventually spent some seven weeks in Syria. Its report did not please Britain and France, but by the time it was published Wilson was dead, and the US Congress had failed to ratify the Treaty of Versailles.

From then on the US pursued its own diplomatic course, trading on its anti-colonial image and patiently cultivating the rulers of the new Middle East. Its first breakthrough came just before World War II. In 1933 Standard Oil Co of California had signed an exclusive contract with Ibn Saud, king of newly unified Saudi Arabia, to prospect for oil in the kingdom. Five years later, in 1938, the first oil was found there in commercial quantities.

By the end of the Second World War the grip of France and Britain over the Middle East was weakening. As the Cold War developed, the region's vital strategic importance made it a focus of the foreign policies of both the Soviet Union and the United States.

US policy was set out in the Truman Doctrine in 1947. President Harry S Truman proclaimed that the US would support any nation with economic and military aid to prevent it falling under the influence of the Soviet Union. Although much was made of the Soviet threat, the greater fear was of the rise of Arab and Iranian national movements that would want to take control over their oil resources.

Between 1945 and 1958 a series of revolutions swept the Middle East, overturning the regimes put in place during the Mandate era. The primary aims of the new governments were to shake off British and French rule, and to set their countries on the path of economic development.

The watershed for the old colonial powers was the Suez Crisis of 1956. When Egypt nationalised the Suez Canal. Britain and France, in collusion with Israel, launched a short-lived and disastrous invasion of the Canal. They were widely condemned in the Arab world, leaving the US free to step into their place.

The honeymoon was short-lived. In 1958 the US engineered a coup against Dr. Mohammed Mosaddeq, the elected popular nationalist leader in Persia. The same year US Marines landed in Lebanon to check a growing revolt against the western-backed government. Throughout the 1960s the Truman Doctrine led to rising military aid to US allies caught in the regional struggle between nationalist governments and the monarchies.

In 1967 Israel launched a pre-emptive war against Egypt, Jordan and

Conflicts of interest

Though the United States was not without colonial ambitions of its own – e.g., in the Philippines and Puerto Rico – its foreign policy throughout the 20th century was consistently anti-colonial. Thus it was reluctant to enter both World Wars, and when it did, it was on the clear understanding that Britain and France would not be helped to retain, still less increase, their empires. The crunch came in 1956, when the US forced a humiliating halt to their Suez invasion.

The Failure of American Diplomacy

Syria, and within six days neutralised the main threat to western influence in the region. That war proved to the US the importance of Israel. Relations between the two states became firmly fixed. The US would arm and support Israel as a counterbalance to Soviet backed regimes. Similar agreements were concluded with the pro-western monarchies in Saudi Arabia and Persia.

The Middle East was thus divided into two hostile camps: Israel and the pro-western monarchies that owed their existence to the mandate era, and the newly emerging independent republics led, on the whole, by popular nationalist leaders. With every outbreak of conflict between Israel and her neighbours, the anti-colonial image of the US in the region was further damaged. The Americans were perceived, not without reason, always to favour Israeli over Arab interests.

In 1979 the pro-western Shah of Persia was overthrown in a popular Islamic revolution. Persia became the Islamic Republic of Iran. Ayatollah Khomeini, its new leader, denounced all things western. The revolution caused a profound change in Western, and especially US, policy: the Arab regimes, even sworn enemies of Israel, were seen as natural allies against the new and more dangerous threat of non-Arab Iran. When Saddam Hussein took advantage of the turmoil of the revolution to attack Iran, the West provided him liberally with arms and other supplies.

By 1989 the Soviet Union, defeated in Afghanistan, was no longer a serious challenger in the Middle East. Iraq was fatally weakened by its 8-year war with Iran, and later by the First Gulf War.

The US therefore sought to solve the Arab-Israeli conflict and undermine the growing Islamist challenge. The fiery Arab nationalist rhetoric was replaced by a more diplomatic tone, while the cause of anti-imperialism, that had brought many of the regimes to power, became more pragmatic.

Nevertheless, for the vast majority of Arabs democracy and freedom of expression remained a mirage. While dictatorships across Latin America, the Far East and the Soviet Union were swept away by new popular movements, the regimes in the Middle East hung grimly to power and crushed with utter brutality any challenge to their rule. Only the possibility of a US-brokered peace deal between Arabs and Israel created some hope. And some Arab regimes, both pro- and anti-western, fearing the influence of the Iranian revolution, and under intense American pressure, initiated limited steps towards reform.

Any optimism disappeared with the attacks on the US in September 2001. President George Bush introduced a new pre-emptive military policy – leading to the invasions of Afghanistan and Iraq – combined with 'regime change', driven by the belief that unless the region was set on a firm democratic footing, it would remain unstable. With little sign of success in Iraq, a full four years after the invasion, the call for 'widespread consultation' first raised by King-Crane has been raised again.

CHARLES RICHARD CRANE was a wealthy industrialist, an Arabist and, after falling out with the Republicans, a financial supporter of the Democrats. He contributed substantially to Woodrow Wilson's successful presidential campaign in 1912.

While best known for his role in the Commission, Crane was involved, albeit secretly, in two earlier events that helped to shape the 20th century. He financed Sun Yat-Sen's revolution which in 1911 ended the reign of China's last emperor; and he introduced Wilson to Tomas Masaryk, the Czech nationalist. In 1918 Crane and Masaryk together persuaded Wilson to support the break-up of the Austro-Hungarian Empire. Masaryk became the first president of independent Czechoslavakia. In gratitude Crane's elder daughter was depicted on an early Czech stamp. His elder son became the first US ambassador to Czechoslovakia; his younger son married Masaryk's daughter.

Delegates waiting at Serai-Amman to present their cases to the King-Crane Commission in July 1919.

The Arab Dream

Although the King-Crane Commission's recommendations were never implemented, its very existence signified the growing power of the United States which, however, was not ready for the responsibility.

Had the great powers heeded the recommendations set out by King-Crane, the history of the region could have been different. However, none of the advice was taken. And far from providing a brief period of development leading to independence, Britain and France used their mandates to impose direct rule over what they regarded as the 'spoils of war'. Almost immediately they met with serious opposition.

The seeds of revolt were sown before the First World War. In 1913 a group of Arab intellectuals had gathered in Paris to formulate a set of demands for greater autonomy within the Ottoman Empire. They voiced the rising unease at the increased centralisation and 'Turkification' of the empire, and pressed for greater cultural freedom as well as limits on the unpopular conscription into the empire's army.

The group drew on European and American traditions of nations and nation building, and the encounter between western and eastern ideas gave birth to a range of nationalist movements based variously on secular, socialist and Islamist ideals. Their leaders wanted to create structures and institutions to match the increasing development of the region. They evolved the idea of an Arab nation state, a sovereign territory where the citizens would share a common language, culture and values.

What fuelled these new ideas was the breakneck economic development that had started in the 1890s. Egypt and Lebanon were undergoing rapid urbanisation, with a growing and confident middle class. Old industries were being modernised, new ones created. Syria and Iraq were not far behind.

The Ottomans reacted with repression. In 1915 and 1916 they executed a number of Syrian and Lebanese intellectuals. But the deaths of the Martyrs, as they became known, simply served to raise their stature among ordinary people. For the rest of the war the radical nationalist movements supported Britain, on the promise of independence when the fighting ended[5].

The war inflicted poverty and famine on large swathes of the near east. The following recovery was then marked by a huge transfer of national assets into the hands of the colonial companies.

France, facing economic ruin, taxed its colonies to the limit – the Syrian treasury, for example, was emptied to pay for French reconstruction[6]. Also, the new frontiers drawn by the Sykes-Picot agreement destroyed the internal markets. Goods, such as silk and cotton, could no longer flow across the markets of the old Ottoman empire. Industries that before the war had employed hundreds of thousands went into terminal decline. The war and the mandates shattered the dream of economic development, independence and democracy.

Stoking the fire ...

Arab nationalism scarcely existed for most of the 19th century. Such organised protest as there was merely sought greater autonomy within the Ottoman Empire. Arab national awareness was stirred up first by Zionist immigration from the 1890s onwards, then by rapid economic development in the region. During the First World War, harsh measures by the collapsing Empire provoked the birth of a new Arab nationalism, encouraged by British and French promises of independence.

Growing resentment in Arab towns and cities was expressed in nationalist violence. Insurrections broke out in Iraq, Syria and Egypt, and spread to Algeria and Morocco. These uprisings were suppressed, but they served notice on Britain and France that imposing their rule would be a difficult and bloody process.

Revolt began in 1919 in Egypt, which had been under British occupation since 1882. When a delegation of Egyptian politicians, led by Saad Zaghlul, applied for permission to attend the Versailles conference to put the case for independence, the British authorities had them deported to Malta. Their treatment sparked off huge protests across Egypt. The scale of the revolt forced the British to grant Egypt independence. However they imposed an authoritarian monarch – King Fuad – and retained control over Egypt's foreign and defence policy, and the Suez Canal.

To isolate rebellion in the mandate territories, the authorities made an alliance with landowners and introduced limited elections. But the elected representatives had no real power, and their frustration gave rise to a new movement that began to challenge both the mandate authorities and the old social classes.

In the 1930s and 40s a new generation of Arab intellectuals developed a set of nationalist ideas that emphasised the shared history, culture and language of the Arabs, and also, for some, their religion. The most influential of these was Michele Aflaq, founder of the Ba'ath (revival or awakening) party. Aflaq called for a return to the glorious past of the Muslim Empire, with its advances in arts, science and culture. He believed that drawing on this rich tradition could be the basis of a renaissance of the Arab people living under the "shame of colonisation".

The Middle East emerged from the Second World War economically and politically more powerful. A substantial economic boom strengthened the independence movements and, by the 1950s, most of the local leaders promoted by Britain and France were swept away in a wave of nationalist revolutions. Some varieties of nationalism, as in Palestine and Lebanon, rejected the idea of a wider Arab identity. Others – Pan Arabism and Arab Socialism – embraced it and advocated the creation of a single Arab state modelled on the United States. The most vocal proponent of Pan Arabism was Gamal Abdul Nasser, the Egyptian leader who in 1958 formed the short-lived United Arab republic with Syria.

Arab Socialism was championed by Algerian leader Ahmed Ben Bella. He sought to blend elements of Marxism and western Socialist ideals with Arab and Islamic traditions, emphasising the common ownership of property, land redistribution and an economic system modelled on the Soviet Union.

A second current emerged in Egypt in the 1930s. An Islamic lawyer, Hassan al-Banna, the founder of the Muslim Brotherhood. rejected the new secular movements, and took the tradition teachings of the Koran as their guide to national liberation and economic development. Al-Banna's ideas galvanised a new generation of thinkers and activists who sought to revive Islamic traditions that had been in retreat for more than a century.

A third current, communism, reached its height in the 1950s and 1960s. Inspired by the Soviet Union and the Third World revolutions, it put the state control of modernisation and development at the heart of the drive for independence.

Despite their differences, the central theme of all these programmes was that independence would go hand-in-hand with economic development, free of monopolies imposed by outside powers. All industries would be under some form of national control, whether private or state, and the profits used to feed further development. The new institutions would have some form of democratic accountability.

For the first decade of independence the promise appeared to have been fulfilled. But by the early 1970s the dream had faded, and democracy had been replaced by dictatorship, repression and war. From 1980 onwards the Islamists emerged as the dominant opposition, both through the ballot box and by the gun. Six years after 9/11 focused the minds of western powers and the regimes across the Middle East on the urgent need for reform, there are few signs of progress.

Although the son of a middle class Christian family from Syria, Michel Aflaq argued that the heart of the "Arab genius" was its Islamic tradition. He was a fervent supporter of free speech, human rights and democracy, but by the time of his death in 1989, the parties he helped to found in Syria and Iraq had split, and both countries had become dictatorships. His tomb is now enclosed inside the Green Zone in Baghdad, Iraq.

Kuwait and the rise of the woman voter

Before Iraq invaded in 1990, Kuwait was known to the world, if at all, as a repressive, corrupt but rich ally of the West. After liberation, by a US-led international coalition, the ruling al-Sabah family returned from exile to face demands for reform, chief among them the right of women to vote.

In 50 years a tribal society has been transformed into a highly developed modern state. With 10% of the world's oil reserves, Kuwait built infrastructure and services for a population which rose from 75,000 in 1937 to almost three million today. The al-Sabah monarchy controls most of the wealth and power, thanks to strong ties with Britain, which ran Kuwait as a protectorate until independence in 1961.

Political reform had lagged behind. Kuwait is a constitutional monarchy, but the Emir retains the right to appoint the prime minister, dissolve the National Assembly and initiate laws. In 1996 a combination of international pressure and local opposition persuaded the Emir to introduce an elected parliament, the first in a Gulf state.

The National Assembly was dominated at first by religious conservatives, and in 1999 it blocked a decree by the Emir to extend the suffrage to women. Before 2005 only 15% of citizens could vote. Women, the armed forces, and Kuwaitis who had been naturalised for less than 30 years were barred. But as demands for reform gathered momentum, liberals in the parliament began to exploit their right to interrogate ministers and force more government transparency.

In December 2004 Kuwaiti women had their first breakthrough, when Rola Dashti, a respected economist, was voted chair of the professional Economists Society, then still an overwhelmingly male club.

In May 2005, against strong opposition from conservatives, the National Assembly voted to give women the vote, raising the roll of voters from 139,000 to 339,000; a month later, Massouma al-Mubarak, a 57-year-old academic, became the first woman to be appointed a minister. Two women were also appointed to the municipal council, an unelected body that advises the Emir on civic issues.

Women now constitute 53% of the electorate. Together with a new generation of Kuwaitis educated abroad, they form an increasingly powerful and confident liberal constituency. Kuwait joins Bahrain, Oman and Qatar as the only Gulf States to give women the right to vote and stand for public office.

But problems remain. Two-thirds of the population are foreigners, mostly low-wage workers from poor countries. Many have lived in Kuwait for years but have no vote and few rights. There are also around 100,000 Arabs, mostly from other tribes, and a Shi'ite minority, who have been denied citizenship and are excluded from public services, including education and the generous welfare provisions. And the conservative opposition, in alliance with Islamists, have founded a party, the *Hizb al-Umma*, which seeks to reverse the gains made by the liberals.

Egypt since the Revolution

Limited elections have been a feature of three distinct periods of authoritarian government since a coup fronted by General Mohamed Neguib overthrew the monarchy in 1952.

The new military administration's first move was to introduce a very popular land reform act, taking all estates of more than roughly 80,000 hectares from their rich, often absentee, landowners and distributing them to the peasants who worked them. The regime also set out to modernise the Egyptian economy, and agriculture in particular, notably by building the Aswan High Dam on the Nile.

Nasser's role in the subsequent Suez crisis, and Britain's humiliation, greatly enhanced his already growing popularity, and he was encouraged to promise the country a "sound democratic life" with mass participation in national and local decision making. In 1956 he promulgated Law 73, giving the ministry of the interior, provincial security agents and the judiciary the task of ensuring fair elections. He also granted women the vote, and lowered the voting age from 21 to 19. However, in the plebiscite that year to approve a new constitution and elect the president, Nasser was the only candidate, winning with over 99% of the vote. And in 1957 only one party, the National Democratic Party (NDP), was allowed to contest the first legislative elections. Opposition parties, including the Muslim Brotherhood and Communist party, were outlawed or absorbed by the NDP. Independents could stand for regional and legislative elections, but widescale vote rigging ensured the right candidates always won.

Nasser died in September 1970, and was succeeded by another member of the coup, Anwar Sadat. Sadat wrote Law 73 into the constitution, as part of a plan to strengthen the "state of law and institutions". But another unsuccessful war with Israel, and the failure of Nasser's dream of a United Arab Republic, led to renewed discontent which in 1977 turned into a popular uprising and mutinies by soldiers and police. The uprising was eventually crushed, but the warning signs were there: reform or face revolt.

The third period, called the 'March to Democracy', was initiated in 1984 by Husni Mubarak, who became president after Sadat was assassinated by Islamic militants in 1981. A plan by Mubarak for multiparty democracy was, however, undermined by a state of emergency. An Islamic opposition, composed mainly of offshoots of the Muslim Brotherhood, waged a violent campaign against tourists and security forces. Free speech and the right to assembly were both outlawed. The state eventually triumphed, but the pressure for lasting change continued to mount.

Mubarak and his ruling party faced a challenge from two groups: the Muslim Brotherhood and the *Kifaya* (Enough), the Egyptian Movement for Change. The Brotherhood, which traces its history back to the 1930s, has been the mainstay of discontent throughout Egypt's modern history. Kifaya, a new

The army calls the shots

The coup of 1952 came after several months of unrest directed against British occupation of the Canal Zone, and the corrupt pro-British monarchy. Neguib was soon considered too moderate, and was forced out by Lieutenant-Colonel Gamal Abdel Nasser, the real leader of the plotters. For the next four years, government was by strict military rule.

Some of the Egyptian military leaders who led the coup d'etat in Cairo, Egypt, July 31, 1952. From left to right, seated: Lt-Colonel Zacharia Mohieddin; Squadron Leader Hassan Ibrahim; Lt-Colonel Youssef Saddick; Lt-Colonel Anwar Sadat; Wing Commander Aly Baghdady; Lt-Colonel Gamal Abdel Nasser; General Mohamed Neguib and Colonel Ahmed Sawki. Left to right, standing: Major Kamal El Din Hussein and Major Abdel Hakim Amer. (AP Photo) alliance of left wing organisations and adherents of Arab Socialism, known as Nasserism, emerged with the first signs of democratisation. Since 2004 it has taken the lead in galvanising discontent, organising demonstrations and protest meetings.

After the 9/11 attacks on the US, the Bush administration saw Egypt's gradual process of democratisation as a model that could serve for the region. A key ally of the United States, Egypt has been the second largest recipient of US aid in the region after Israel.

The first real test of the 'democratic flowering' came in 2005. In May a referendum was held to allow the first direct, multi-candidate presidential elections. Opposition groups complained, however, that the referendum was held after voter registration had closed, effectively disenfranchising a large segment ot the population. Mubarak faced one challenger: Ayman Nour of the Ghad Party. Nour received less than 10% of the vote and was later jailed for alleged forgery.

The parliamentary elections set for November and December of the same year proved even more contentious. There were significant gains for opposition parties, including the banned Muslim Brotherhood who stood as independents. The polls were marked by widespread violence and voter intimidation: riot police prevented voters from casting their ballot in areas where the opposition looked like winning seats. Deep suspicion of ballot rigging and electoral manipulation is undermining popular support for democracy: the Arab world's largest nation is unlikely to tolerate more broken promises.

After 30 years of military rule, the greatest champions for free elections have emerged from the most unlikely place, the judiciary. Since 1984 judges have personally monitored polling stations. In the local elections of 2002 the judges demanded the right to oversee the 37,410 'auxiliary polling stations'. Opposition groups claimed these were being used to fix the vote and they boycotted the elections. Many judges claimed that their colleagues were intimidated after they reported electoral fraud. They called on the army to protect them after allegedly being threatened by security forces and supporters of the ruling NDP.

For the 2005 elections the Judges' Club announced that it would exorcise the 'stigma of elections' and charged two high court judges, Mahmud Mekki and Hisham Bastawisi, with the task of investigating vote rigging. Their report detailed widespread fraud, and accused some fellow judges of complicity in the ballot rigging. They were hauled before a disciplinary committee and accused of slander – a charge that could have seen them disbarred. Their court case became the focus for opposition groups who, despite intimidation, held regular protests near the court in central Cairo.

On the first day of the trial, in April 2006, more than 300 judges attempted to enter the courtroom to observe the proceedings, while up to 7,000 of Egypt's 9,000 judges campaigned together to end government interference in the judiciary. This normally conservative body thus found itself at the centre of a wider campaign for reform, a move unprecedented in Egypt's modern history. On the eve of the trial Bastawisi said, "[The people] want a clean judiciary, free and fair elections, and the judges are expressing these views".

Local protest and international pressure resulted in Bastawisi receiving a reprimand while Mekki had all charges against him dropped. The decision was seen as a victory for the movement and a step towards real democratic change.

Kifaya, too, has been at the centre of demands for political reform in Egypt. It called for a boycott of the elections, saying that widespread fraud and intimidation made the result inevitable. The Muslim Brotherhood, on the other hand, urged Egyptians to vote even though its candidates were barred from standing.

The majority of Egyptians heeded the call for a boycott. According to official figures, only 22% of Egypt's 32 million registered voters took part in the poll. Democracy campaigners claim the turnout was much lower, with 12% in rural areas and only 5% in the cities. The Egyptian Organisation for Human Rights, which helped monitor some polling stations, said that 15% of votes cast were "questionable". Opponents accused Mubarak supporters of stuffing ballot boxes. Others complained that they turned up to vote only to discover they were 'not registered'. More than 500 judges were banned from overseeing the poll after they called for full transparency in the election.

The rise of the reformists comes at a time of growing discontent against the regime's neo-liberal policies.

Egyptian voters used ladders to get into a polling station in Bosat, a town 160 km north of Cairo, when their polling station was blocked by anti-riot police during the final round of Egypt's parliamentary vote in December 2005. (AP Photo/Amr Nabil)

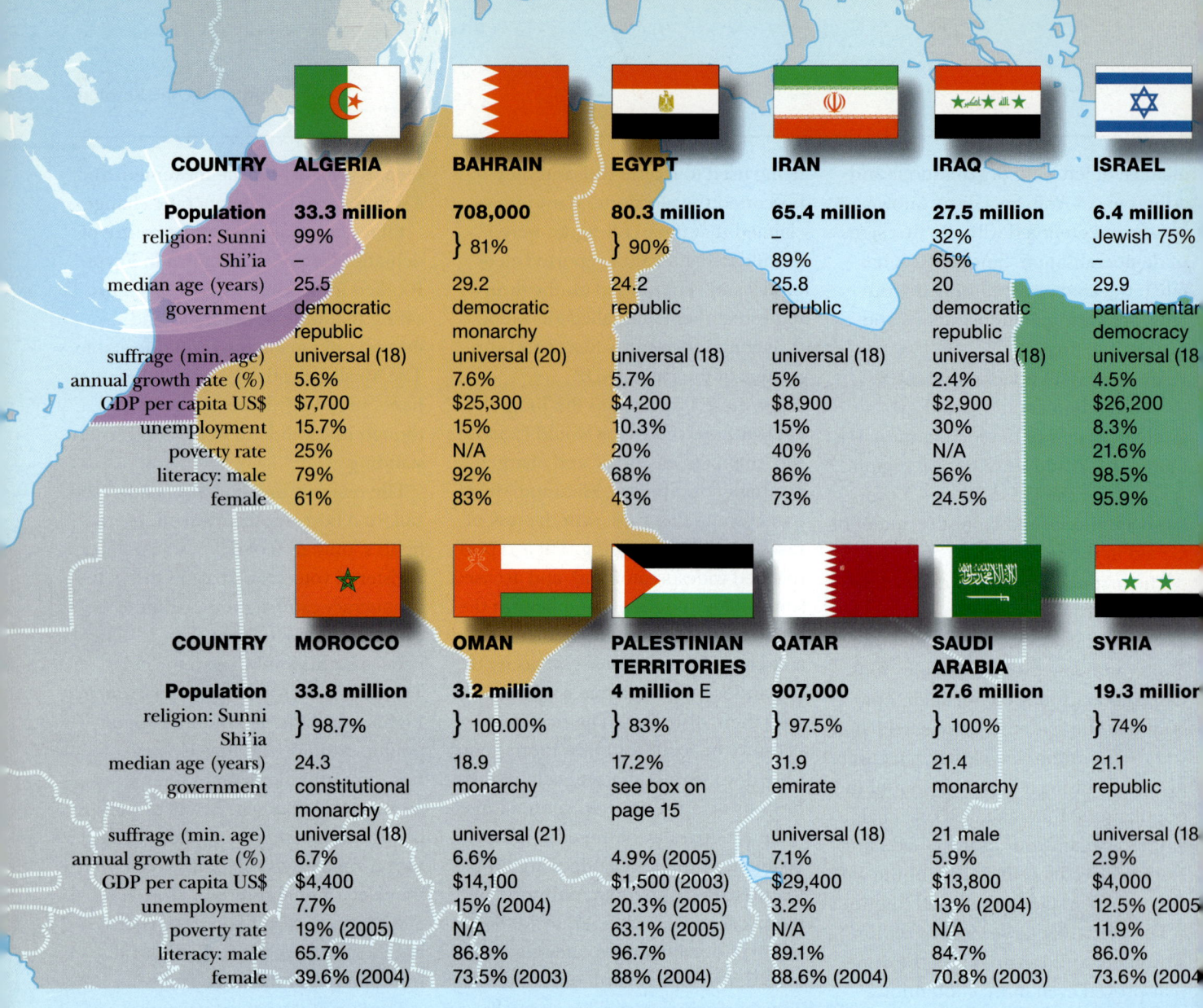

COUNTRY	ALGERIA	BAHRAIN	EGYPT	IRAN	IRAQ	ISRAEL
Population	33.3 million	708,000	80.3 million	65.4 million	27.5 million	6.4 million
religion: Sunni	99%	} 81%	} 90%	–	32%	Jewish 75%
Shi'ia	–			89%	65%	–
median age (years)	25.5	29.2	24.2	25.8	20	29.9
government	democratic republic	democratic monarchy	republic	republic	democratic republic	parliamentary democracy
suffrage (min. age)	universal (18)	universal (20)	universal (18)	universal (18)	universal (18)	universal (18)
annual growth rate (%)	5.6%	7.6%	5.7%	5%	2.4%	4.5%
GDP per capita US$	$7,700	$25,300	$4,200	$8,900	$2,900	$26,200
unemployment	15.7%	15%	10.3%	15%	30%	8.3%
poverty rate	25%	N/A	20%	40%	N/A	21.6%
literacy: male	79%	92%	68%	86%	56%	98.5%
female	61%	83%	43%	73%	24.5%	95.9%

COUNTRY	MOROCCO	OMAN	PALESTINIAN TERRITORIES	QATAR	SAUDI ARABIA	SYRIA
Population	33.8 million	3.2 million	4 million E	907,000	27.6 million	19.3 million
religion: Sunni	} 98.7%	} 100.00%	} 83%	} 97.5%	} 100%	} 74%
Shi'ia						
median age (years)	24.3	18.9	17.2%	31.9	21.4	21.1
government	constitutional monarchy	monarchy	see box on page 15	emirate	monarchy	republic
suffrage (min. age)	universal (18)	universal (21)		universal (18)	21 male	universal (18)
annual growth rate (%)	6.7%	6.6%	4.9% (2005)	7.1%	5.9%	2.9%
GDP per capita US$	$4,400	$14,100	$1,500 (2003)	$29,400	$13,800	$4,000
unemployment	7.7%	15% (2004)	20.3% (2005)	3.2%	13% (2004)	12.5% (2005)
poverty rate	19% (2005)	N/A	63.1% (2005)	N/A	N/A	11.9%
literacy: male	65.7%	86.8%	96.7%	89.1%	84.7%	86.0%
female	39.6% (2004)	73.5% (2003)	88% (2004)	88.6% (2004)	70.8% (2003)	73.6% (2004)

KEY TO MAP

■ Democracy ■ Monarchy ■ Republic ■ Others

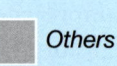

'Democratic' and 'universal suffrage' in the table above have widely different meanings and limits in the different countries. In almost all, they are tempered by a greater or lesser degree of authoritarian control. In the extreme case of Saudi Arabia, for example, the constitution treats the wealth of the state as belonging to the ruling Al-Saud family and democratic reform has so far been limited to local councils and issues. Women are still not allowed to drive cars.

However, it should not be assumed that the democracy increasingly demanded in Arab countries is the market-driven, socially liberal democratic style of the West. Many Arabs despise the lax attitudes, high crime rates and low voter participation they see in so many Western countries. Their challenge is to find their own style of democracy, combining greater 'people power' and more equality of opportunity, especially between the sexes, with the best of their Islamic traditions.

All figures are for 2006 or 2007 except where stated
Literacy = % of population aged 15 and over able to read and write
E = Estimated

Percentage rise in internet usage between 2...

Unsurprisingly, the more westernized countries of the highest penetration of internet usage, with Isra growth figures are striking, especially those for Ira Syria, three of the most authoritarian regimes in re and the media. As internet connections in these co

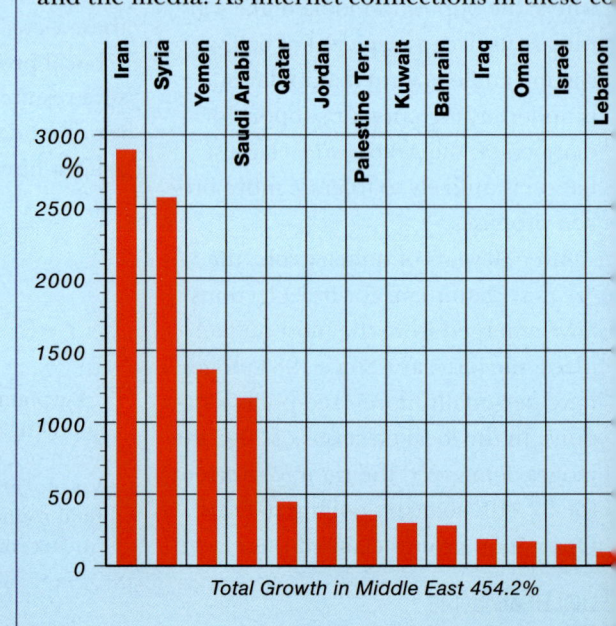

Iran | Syria | Yemen | Saudi Arabia | Qatar | Jordan | Palestine Terr. | Kuwait | Bahrain | Iraq | Oman | Israel | Lebanon

Total Growth in Middle East 454.2%

Democracy in the Arab World

	KUWAIT	LEBANON
...million	2.5 million	3.9 million
	70%	} 59.7%
	30%	
	26	28.3
...itutional ...rchy	constitutional emirate	republic
...sal (18)	universal (20)	universal (21)
	8.0%	~5%
	$21,600	$5,500
...(30%)	2.2% (2004)	20%
...(2001)	N/A	28% (1999)
	94.4%	93.1%
	91.0%	82.2% (2003)

	UAE	YEMEN
...million E	4.4 million	22.2 million
...%	} 96%	} muslim (maj)
	30.1	16.7
...blic	federal	republic
...sal (20)	none	universal (18)
	10.2%	3.2%
	$49,700	$900
	2.4% (2001)	35% (2003)
(2005)	N/A	45.2% (2003)
	76.1%	70.5%
(2004)	81.7% (2003)	30% (2003)

Al Jazeera

An important symbol of the changing political landscape in the Arab world is the satellite television station Al Jazeera.

Al Jazeera – Arabic for island or peninsula – is based in the Gulf state of Qatar. It was started in 1996 by a group of former BBC Arabic journalists. It broke new ground as the first Arabic news station to broadcast real journalism and debate, in contrast to the turgid propaganda and staid programming offered by state-run channels across the Arab world. It has aired debates with Israeli officials, breaking a taboo in Arab broadcasting.

The channel is funded by the Emir of Qatar, Shaikh Hamid al-Thani, using his income from the country's vast oil and gas reserves. Many Arab states see it as threatening, and their relations with the Qatari government have soured further with each critical programme. The channel's reporters are banned from some Arab countries, including Iraq.

More recently the US and other western governments have accused Al Jazeera of encouraging terrorism by airing videos of the al-Qaida leader Osama bin Ladin, and debates critical of Washington's policies in the Arab world. Supporters say it practises legitimate journalism and that airing bin Ladin videos is something any news station would do, given the opportunity. Qatar has close ties with the US and has a large American airbase. It is under pressure from the US to tone down reporting from the station.

Since Al Jazeera first took to the airways many other independent satellite channels have sprung up across the region.

Al Jazeera's popularity has spread across the globe, and it has recently launched "Al Jazeera English ... the world's first English language news channel to be headquartered in the Middle East. Broadcasting from within the Middle East, looking outwards".

2005

...East show ...0%. But the ...rabia and ...roadcasting ...ether ...andestine, in ...rivate houses, ...r public, in ...ternet cafes, ...ublic libraries ...c., are likely ...o be widely ...ared, figures ...r pentration ...e probably ...nderestimated ...nd, given the ...pid growth ...n all three ...ountries, ...ill soon be ...perceded.

Press freedom in the Middle East

Of 167 countries worldwide, North Korea has the least freedom of the press, northern European countries the most. Satellite TV, the internet, and freedom to travel mean that thinking citizens of Arab countries are quite well informed.

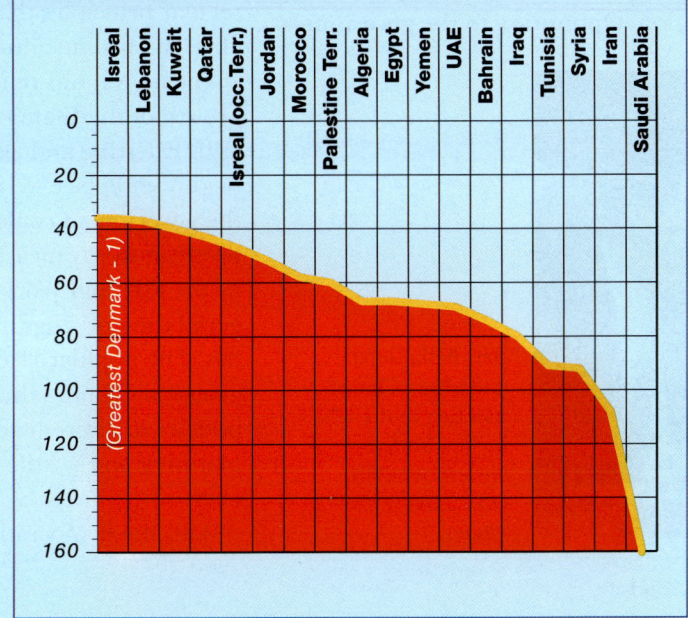

(Greatest Denmark - 1)

Countries ranked: Isreal, Lebanon, Kuwait, Qatar, Isreal (occ.Terr.), Jordan, Morocco, Palestine Terr., Algeria, Egypt, Yemen, UAE, Bahrain, Iraq, Tunisia, Syria, Iran, Saudi Arabia

Sources: Internet Marketing Stats, Miniwatts Marketing Group, CIA World Factbook 2007, etc.

Algeria, From the Rifle to the Ballot Box

Algeria is Africa's second largest country. After being conquered from the Ottoman Empire by France in 1830, large numbers of French settlers - the pieds noirs *- moved in.*

The first president of independent Algeria, Ahmed Ben Bella, capitalised on Algeria's standing in the Middle East by transforming it into an important centre of Arab nationalism. Popular hopes were high as Ben Bella set out a path of national development modelled on socialist state planning; not least, the new government planned to disband the FLN in favour of a multi-party democracy.

Such hopes were dashed in June 1965 when Houari Boumédienne, one of the military commanders of the FLN, seized power and declared himself president. The coup ended the honeymoon between the FLN and the population. Ben Bella was exiled.

Boumédienne remodelled the state, giving the military a central role in running the country. From 1965 until his death in December 1978, Algeria was a one-party state with limited public participation in decision making. Throughout the 1970s, despite the discovery of important gas reserves, the economy stagnated and many of the gains made during the years of economic development gave way to austerity measures imposed by the IMF and the World Bank.

From colony to nation

Opposition by indigenous Algerians to French rule and the settlers was led by a popular Islamic independence movement, the National Liberation Front (FLN). In a bloody civil war from 1954 to 1962 an estimated 500,000 died (out of a population of 8 million). The violence spread to mainland France. The conflict was only ended when French president de Gaulle accepted the inevitable, and granted Algeria independence in 1962.

After Boumédienne's death in 1979, two candidates challenged for the presidency: Abdelaziz Bouteflika, a rising star within the FLN, and Chadli Bendjedid, the candidate of the military. Bendjedid prevailed, and Bouteflika was forced into exile.

Bendjedid ruled in a troubled decade that saw the failure of many state-sponsored economic projects. In October 1988 rising discontent exploded in mass rioting influenced by the Islamic revivalism sweeping the region. Opposition to the government rallied behind a new party, the Islamic Salvation Front, known by the French acronym FIS.

The president responded by setting out plans for multi-party democracy. He hoped to draw the Islamist sting by co-opting the FIS into a loyal opposition. But his gamble failed when the Islamists swept the 1991 parliamentary elections. It seemed that they were on the point of gaining power by the democratic route, and that the elections would become a model for the region. With the FLN humiliated at the polls, the military, backed by France, annulled the election results and outlawed the Islamist party.

Arab nationalists feared that an Islamist government would set back Algeria's development, at the heart of which had been secular ideals. The achievements of the independence movement were, however, lost on a new generation who felt that any social and economic development had passed them by. The Islamist revival of the late 1970s and 1980s was partly a reaction to broken promises of economic improvements, but also reflected hostility to the government's secular principles that were seen as alien to Muslim culture.

The revival was reinforced by the growth of the Islamic charities that, as in Palestine and elsewhere, had begun to replace welfare programmes the government could not afford. The severe austerity measures required by the IMF and World Bank had triggered the uprisings in the 1970s and 80s. The popular Islamist opposition groups attributed the failed economic policies to discredited secular socialist planning and hostile foreign interference.

With the democratic road blocked,

Ben Bella (left) and Hugo Chavez meeting at the UN in New York in November 2001. (REUTERS/Kimberly White)

the FIS launched an armed insurgency marked by brutality and the massacre of many innocent people by both the insurgents and state forces. An estimated 150,000 lives were lost during this second 10-year civil war.

In 1994 Bendjedid was replaced by another general, Liamine Zéroual. The new ruler vowed to crush the insurgency and restart, once again, the democratic process. He legalised opposition parties and launched a series of elections between November 1995 and October 1997.

The elections did nothing to calm the insurgency. The Islamists rejected any form of participation and declared their opposition to a democratic process they considered both corrupt and corrupting. The polls were marked by ballot rigging and gerrymandering. Meanwhile large parts of the country fell under the control of the FIS and the more radical offshoot, the Armed Islamic Group.

The insurgents opted for a harsh interpretation of Sharia law in the areas under their control. Their arbitrary application of these laws, and severe punishment of those who opposed their policies, eventually undermined their popular support. The civil war became a bloody stalemate. By April 1999 Zéroual admitted failure and stepped aside in favour of Abdelaziz Bouteflika.

Bouteflika returned from exile with the promise to "put out the fires" and revive the fortunes of the country. He went to the polls that year, securing the backing of the military and 74% of the voters for a peace initiative. At the heart of the plan was the restoration of democracy and an amnesty for insurgents and those in the military involved in human rights abuses.

But the years of war and electoral manipulation took their toll on popular participation in the democratic process. The 2002 elections, slated as the most important in the country's history, recorded the lowest turnout since independence – according to official figures only 46%, compared to 65% in 1997. Some observers put the turnout as low as 20%.

However, the democratic initiative succeeded in dividing the Islamists. A new party, the Movement for National Reform, moderated its demands. It agreed to support economic restraints charted by global financial institutions and to adhere to strict foreign policies dictated by the military. In return the party was free to campaign for the Islamisation of Algerian society. One of the main demands was tougher cultural restraints on the country's large ethnic Berber minority.

Faced with a disenchanted Arab Algeria and a new rebellion among the Berbers in the Kabylie (see box), Bouteflika struggled to convince the country that his plan for democracy was real. However in April 2004 he stood for a second term, and secured 85% of the vote in an election widely regarded as free and fair.

The elections gave Bouteflika the mandate, and legitimacy, to reach out to the Islamists. He negotiated an end to the insurgency and agreed an amnesty for those who laid down their weapons. His National Reconciliation Plan, approved by a general referendum in 2005, marked the final chapter of the bloody conflict.

Algeria's failed experiments with one party rule, Islamist insurgency and corrupt democratic process has hampered the emergence of a stable democratic system, but peace has brought dividends. The ballot box has replaced the bullet; the military elite have accepted that political legitimacy can only come through popular mandate. Problems remain however, the tensions in the Kabylie could, once again, lead to renewed violence and division.

The Berber revolt

The national reconciliation plan dowsed the flames of war in Arab Algeria, but lit a fuse in the Kabylie, the historic homeland of the Berbers in the mountains and areas east of Algiers. The region rose in revolt in 2001 after a young Berber, Massinissa Guermah, was killed while in the custody of the national police. His death sparked the longest wave of rioting in Algeria's modern history. The Kabylie region, unsympathetic to the Islamist insurgency, maintained long-standing demands for cultural and social autonomy from central government.

The rioting culminated in a million-strong demonstration in June 2001 through the capital Algiers. The government ordered the army and police into the streets, claiming the movement was an ethnic uprising against Arabs. Over 50 people were killed in a crackdown that followed.

The Berbers' cultural demands date back to the eve of Algeria's independence movement. Throughout the 1960s they were limited to calls for autonomy. In 1980 frustration at the lack of progress gave birth to a new, younger and more vocal opposition known as the Berber Spring, whose central demand was for Tamazight, the Berber language, to be given equal and official recognition with Arabic.

Most Algerians are descended from the Berbers, the original inhabitants of North Africa. As the region became Arabised the Kabylie clung to its identity. Sympathy for Berber cultural rights remains high across the country.

Bouteflika's ploy to divide the Berbers from the rest of the country backfired as Arab regions joined the popular uprising, raising their own demands – often over the allocation of resources. "Nous sommes tous Kabylie" (we are all Kabylie) was chanted in Arab towns and villages that summer.

By early autumn the uprising had become a popular movement, as grassroots representatives of tribes and popular committees, local officials and district authorities—known as the Co-ordination of 'Arush, Da'irat and Communes—took effective control of Berber affairs. The government maintained control over the national police and the army.

The Berbers boycotted the 2002 elections.

Jordan and Syria: a Cold Spring

Jordan and Syria, although traditional rivals, have both attempted to co-opt powerful Islamist opponents and diffuse opposition to unpopular policies.

Jordan is one of several Arab countries with no oil or gas reserves. Sandwiched between Iraq, Syria and Saudi Arabia to the east and a powerful Israel to its west, the kingdom has struggled to make economic progress. With one in three of the population living below the poverty line, the Jordanian economy relies on tourism and remittances from emigrants, both of which are hostage to regional tensions.

Jordan's democratic process began in 1989 in response to the widespread discontent caused by an IMF economic adjustment programme. The reforms gave limited political participation to an elected national assembly in return for public acceptance of economic reform. The chief beneficiaries of this partial democracy were the moderate Islamists gathered around the Islamic Action Front which, fearing widespread disorder, sought to become an acceptable peaceful outlet for discontent. The opposition could air grievances over some policies, but steered clear of criticising the king. Foreign policy remained the king's exclusive preserve, in particular the alignment of Jordan's interests with those of the US and its allies in the region.

Yet even this limited programme was blown off course during the First Gulf War (1990-91) and the international sanctions on Iraq, Jordan's key export market. Close economic relations with Saddam Hussein's Iraq had resulted in low fuel prices and a major market for Jordan's goods. The effects of the sanctions on its economy limited the space for economic and political reforms, while democracy within such narrow boundaries proved illusory.

Political reform took another blow after the king signed a peace agreement with Israel in 1994. The deal was highly unpopular in a country with a large population of displaced Palestinians, and it finally put a halt to the democratic experiment.

Discontent surfaced again in August 1996, when a worldwide hike in the price of wheat left the government with little choice but to cut subsidies on bread. Violent protests erupted across the Kingdom. The Islamist opposition were quick to denounce the rioters, and the king responded with a massive crackdown. According to one commentator: "Liberalisation was intended to invite more guests into the living room for 'coffee talk', with a few welcome to stay for dinner. None were to be invited into the kitchen, though, and certainly none were welcome in the rest of the house".

King Hussein's successor, Abdullah II, once again held out the prospect of reform, signalling a new momentum for democracy. But every step towards

Wisdom amidst conflict

Jordan was ruled for 46 years by the Hashemite King Hussein until his death in 1999. This pro-western monarch steered his vulnerable and unfavoured country with great skill through many crises, especially the violent disruption caused by the repeated influx of Arab refugees that followed each war with Israel.

Amman, November 2005. Jordanian students demonstrating during a rally at Jordanian University in support of the King and government. An Iraqi woman had confessed on television that she and her husband had attempted a suicide bombing in an Amman hotel, one of three attacks in the same week in which more than 50 people were killed.
(REUTERS/Ali Jarekji)

The Struggle for Democracy in the Arab World

liberalisation brought with it new restrictions on liberty. And critics claim that managed, gerrymandered constituencies have resulted in the more conservative areas being over-represented in parliament. The parliamentary elections originally scheduled for 2000 were delayed, while a prominent critic of the regime, Toujan al-Faisal, was jailed for attacking corruption.

In 2002 King Abdullah issued an edict further restricting the right to assembly and freedom of the press. The decree came as the region witnessed the biggest demonstrations since the 1950s. Millions of people descended into the streets across the Middle East to protest against the Israeli invasion of the West Bank, and the imprisonment of the Palestinian leader Yasser Arafat in his Ramallah compound.

Jordan found itself hostage to events outside its control. Tens of thousands of students across the kingdom battled riot police, while the Palestinian camps erupted in anger. The protests subsided, but there are more dark clouds on the horizon. After the US, one of the country's major sponsors, invaded Iraq in March 2003 elections were again delayed. The disorder over the border threatens to spill over into Jordan. In 2005 al-Qaida launched a series of attacks inside the kingdom, the bloodiest of which targeted wedding guests in an Amman hotel.

The impact of economic liberalisation has had other, unforeseen, consequences. Traditionally, the private sector was dominated by Palestinians, while the public sector remained the privilege of native Jordanians. Under privatisation state enterprises have been hived off, often to private individuals who emerged out of the bureaucracy. Large numbers of native Jordanians have entered the private sector exacerbating the historic ethnic tensions between the two communities. And this instability has been further fuelled by the arrival of tens of thousands of Iraqis fleeing occupation, insurgency and civil war.

Jordan's stop-start democracy has created some stability. A loyal opposition could be relied on during times of tension, while the halting steps towards mass participation have produced some room for dissent. The national assembly is far from a toothless talking shop: it has repeatedly embarrassed the government by threatening votes of no confidence in ministers. Nevertheless, according to Amnesty International and other human rights organisations the price of dissent in Jordan is high.

Syria: fading spring

Since the death of Hafiz al-Assad in 2000, Syria has experienced a series of false springs. Assad and his socialist Baath Party ruled with an iron grip for 30 years, maintaining tight state control over the economy and firmly suppressing internal opposition.

During the Cold War Syria became a key regional player with the backing of the Soviet Union. But a series of disastrous wars with Israel, including the loss of the Golan Heights in 1967, kept it in a state of permanent crisis.

On succeeding his father as President in 2000, Bashar al-Assad promised political and economic reforms in the hope of creating more stability. These measures, which had been demanded by opponents of the regime, came to be known as the Damascus Spring. Bashar replaced the old guard with new, younger leaders and encouraged criticism of corruption and inefficiency, in order to push out officials who were blocking his programme. Opposition, though mainly confined to intellectual discussion circles, quickly fell foul of the powerful security services. Its key leaders have been jailed, including prominent businessmen and legislators. However, the popular Muslim Brotherhood remains a potent threat to the regime's stability.

In March 2005 Syria withdrew its 16,000 troops from Lebanon. This humiliating retreat has weakened Syria's regional role, and reinforced its international isolation. But the label "state sponsor of terror" keeps it in the sights of both the US and Israel.

With limited and dwindling oil reserves, the Syrian economy continues to stagnate. An estimated 30% of the population live below the poverty line and a lack of investment puts a strain on the crumbling infrastructure. Faced with growing international hostility the regime is trying to soften internal dissent by a process of decentralisation. The commitment to state planning has been dropped and key state-owned industries have been privatised.

Since his accession, Bashar has cleared out the last of the old guard, but the changes have not spread beyond the corridors of power. Dissent is still heavily repressed, and the much vaunted push to political pluralism has failed to materialise.

With enemies on every border, the ruling party is reluctant to ease its grip on power lest it is swept away on a wave of discontent, or becomes another candidate for US-led regime change.

Right to left: Mofti Ahmad Hasoun, President Bashar al-Assad and Minister of Religious Affairs (Aeqaf) Mohammed Ziyad al-Ayoubi, attending prayers during Eid al-Adha at Hafez Assad Mosque in Damascus, on 30th December, 2006. (AP Photo/Sana)

Democratic Revolutions

For more than 30 years after World War II, the Lebanon was the white hope of Middle East democracy. Beirut was called the Paris of the Middle East.

After Lebanon won independence from France in 1943 it adopted the 'national pact', an agreement that guaranteed political representation to all its many religious sects. Government posts were allocated according to sect, with key posts for the major communities. The president was to be a Maronite, the prime minister a Sunni Muslim, the speaker of the house a Shi'ite, the minister of the interior a Greek Orthodox and so on. Parliamentary seats were distributed to ensure a Christian majority according to demographic statistics from the country's only census, conducted in 1932.

Following the foundation of Israel in 1948 tens of thousands of Palestinian refugees, mainly Sunnis, flooded into the country. They were placed in overcrowded camps that became centres of instability. Before long Lebanese politics were riven by different sectarian interests and political philosophies. Some wanted closer relations with the west; others were inspired by the Arab nationalist revolutions sweeping the region. In 1958, a political crisis sparked the first civil war, the 'revolt of the pashas'. That was ended by the intervention of US marines.

During the 1960s a rising social movement, combining communists, socialists and Arab nationalists and radical Palestinian groups, demanded changes in the country's direction. The movement's main challenge was through the ballot box, with a strong showing in the 1969 and 1973 elections. Demographic changes meant that Muslims, too, began to challenge the national pact, and to demand a redistribution of political power.

In 1975 the national consensus collapsed into civil war. The following year Syrian troops entered the country,

> **A very diverse community**
>
> *Lebanon has the most diverse population in the Middle East – every shade of Muslim: Shi'ites, Sunnis, Alawites and Druze; and Christian: Maronite, Catholic, Greek Orthodox, Melkite, Assyrians, Copts, the Armenian churches, – wuth no one group having an absolute majority. Democratic government has always been difficult to achieve.*

with US blessing, to block a victory by the left and secular movements. Israeli troops invaded in 1978, and again in 1982, to drive out Palestinian guerrillas. Throughout the 1980s, the country was fragmented into mini fiefdoms run by private militias. The factions finally agreed a peace treaty in 1990 and the parliamentary seats were redistributed to give the Muslims more proportionate political representation.

Two problems remained. In the south, Israeli troops continued to hold a swathe of the territory captured in 1978, and fought a ten-year war against Hizbollah guerrillas. Elsewhere, more than 16,000 Syrian troops maintained key bases and a firm grip on local politics. The Israelis finally withdrew in 2000, but the Syrian troops stayed.

As recently as 2005, Lebanon was lauded for the way it had emerged from the civil war. In the ensuing fifteen years Beirut had once again become a centre of tourism, the country was rebuilt and people who had fled their homes returned. If Iraq was hoped to be a model of regime change through military intervention, Lebanon was equally held up as a model of change from within. Both countries face similar political, religious and sectarian divisions that threaten to derail a fragile democracy. But in Lebanon the gun appeared to have been removed from political life.

This optimism was shattered on 14 February 2005 when a massive car bomb killed former prime minister Rafiq Hariri and 20 companions. Within six weeks an unprecedented mass movement, known in the West as the 'Cedar Revolution' and in Lebanon as the 'Liberation' Revolution, brought down the government.

The US saw the revolution as a vindication of its drive for democracy across the region, and similar to the 'velvet' revolutions that had swept through the former USSR – largely non-violent protests that had toppled unpopular regimes and produced pro-Western governments. But many Lebanese of all persuasions blamed in turn Arab governments, Israel and the West for exploiting the divisions inside the country. They wanted an end to foreign influence over the country's affairs. Unable to match the military spending of their neighbours, successive governments adopted a policy of 'strength through weakness' and tried to remain neutral. Military weakness kept Lebanon out of the successive Arab-Israeli wars.

Before his death, Hariri, a self-made billionaire who was twice prime minister, had confronted Damascus over the reappointment of his rival, the pro-Syrian Emile Lahoud, as president. After his murder, massive demonstrations in Beirut demanded that Syria relinquish its grip over the country. At the height of the protests, around one million people (out of a population of 3.8 million) took part. Counter demonstrations of equal size also gathered, and for a several weeks the country was split between pro- and anti-Syrian camps. Under massive pressure from Arab governments, the United Nations, and the mass protests, Syria finally withdrew it troops in April 2005. Unpopular as they had been, the Syrians were credited by many people with having provided the security which made it possible to bring the civil war to an end.

After the Cedar Revolution Lebanon held its first fully free elections since 1970. Saad al-Hariri, son of the former prime minister, led a victorious list that brought together one-time civil war foes in a government considered friendly to the West. The opposition was formed by Hizbollah, Syrian backed parties and the leading Christian anti-Syrian politician Michael Aoun.

The Israeli occupation left a lasting legacy on the Shia Muslims, who were the country's largest sect, and possibly an absolute majority of the population. The Shias had originally welcomed the end of PLO control over the south, but twenty-two years of Israeli occupation had radicalised what was the poorest and weakest section of Lebanese society.

Hizbollah was born in the chaos of the 1982 Israeli invasion. When Israel failed to pull out, a fledgling Hizbollah party launched an effective guerrilla war, including kidnappings and suicide bombings. Its role in organising resistance in the south transformed it. Throughout the 1990s the party put much effort into building hospitals and schools, replacing the welfare system that had collapsed during the civil war. Over time it moderated its more radical demands and, while fighting an increasingly successful war in the south, it campaigned strongly on social and environmental issues. After Israel's withdrawal in 2000 the party under its charismatic leader, Sayyed Hassan Nasrallah, became a key player in national politics, contesting elections and securing two government ministries. Yet it remained an implacable enemy of Israel and US policy in the region, and the two countries determined to crush the organisation that had humiliated them.

The war in July 2006 was devastating for Lebanon. Israeli warplanes, gunboats and artillery may have intended to target only Hizbollah areas, but Sunni Muslim and Christian areas were also hit. Much of the new infrastructure was destroyed, as Israel vowed to "push the country back 20 years". The Israelis hoped to re-ignite sectarian conflict, but their campaign backfired. The country reacted by rallying round the Shias. Refugees were welcomed into Christian, Druze and Sunni areas; politicians of all sects vowed to confront Israel.

In spring 2007, smouldering unrest among the 250,000 Palestinians in the refugee camps – who have no vote and no access to state education or health services – has turned into open warfare with the Lebanese army. Lebanon's troubles are not over.

Palestine: When democracy is not enough

The government of the autonomous Palestinian Territories is arguably the most truly democratic administration in the Arab world, despite the fact that the fragmented areas it governs cannot be described as a proper state.

The 1994 Oslo peace agreement between the Palestinian Liberation Organisation (PLO) and Israel gave autonomy to Palestinians living in Gaza and parts of West Bank. The Palestinian National Authority (PNA) was to be an interim governing body for five years, while the terms of a final settlement between Israel and the Palestinians were worked out. The PLO remained the Palestinians' official representative internationally. However, Israel continued to occupy large parts of the autonomous territories and to built illegal settlements. This has deepened the divisions among the Palestinians: to simplify, Hamas, a militant Islamist party, denies Israel's right to exist, while Fatah, the largest component of the PLO, is a secular movement that seeks to negotiate a two-state solution.

Presidential and parliamentary elections for the PNA took place in 1996. Fatah won and Yasser Arafat, founder of Fatah, became president. The next elections were scheduled for 2001, but were delayed after the start of the second Intifada. Arafat died in 2004 and was succeeded by Mahmoud Abbas.

In 2006 new legislative elections were held and Hamas won with 44% of the vote, creating new tensions between a Hamas administration and a Fatah president. The US and the EU consider Hamas a terrorist group because it targets Israeli civilians as part of its 'war of resistance' against the occupation. However popular its stance, Hamas's victory was mostly a reaction to Fatah's corruption and poor governance. As the economy deteriorated, with more people living in poverty, Hamas had set up its own welfare programmes including schools and clinics.

Following the election, Israel withheld the $55 million that it collects through customs duties. The EU and US also halted their aid to the PNA - in 2005 this had been over $1 billion. Critics say this policy was part of a plan to starve the PNA of funding so that it could not govern effectively, thus diminishing Hamas' popularity among Palestinian voters.

The lack of funding has indeed created severe hardship in some areas of the Palestinian-governed territories. The result has been renewed rocket attacks by Hamas on Israel, and something close to civil war between Hamas and Fatah.

For the West, Hamas's election victory was an embarrassment. The US administration in particular vocally promotes democracy as the cure for the region's problems, but its reaction to Hamas's success seems to show that it will not accept democratically elected governments opposed to US policies.

Yet opinion polls conducted after the elections revealed that voters were primarily concerned with good governance. "In the estimate of 52% of the respondents, Fatah lost the elections because voters wanted first and foremost to punish it for the spread of corruption. A further 19% attribute the loss to Fatah's divisions and lack of leadership, 17% to its failure to put an end to anarchy. Only 5% attributed it to the failure of the peace process." (www.pcpsr.org/survey/polls/2006/p19e.html)

Additional Notes

1 Mandates

The Mandates were created by the Treaty of Versailles to provide for the future of the subject territories of the defeated powers, essentially Germany and the Ottoman Empire. They were to be of short duration and to be supervised by the League of Nations. The precise terms of each mandate depended on the degree of development in the territory and its readiness for independence. Thus Iraq became an independent monarchy as early as 1922, albeit with continuing strong ties to Britain, while Palestine remained mandate territory until 1948, when Britain withdrew exhausted.

In the absence of the US, Britain and France dominated the League of Nations, and it was widely thought at the time that the mandate territories were mere colonies by another name. Both countries had been impoverished by the costs of the war, and Britain in particular ended it with huge debts to the US for materiel it had received on credit. Not unnaturally, defeat of the Ottomans would make their territories and oil wealth forfeit to the victors.

2 The Sykes-Picot Agreement

This secret understanding between Britain and France, made in winter 1915/6, set out their future spheres of interest in the Middle East after the expected defeat of the Ottoman Empire. The negotiators, Georges Picot and Sir Mark Sykes, were both Catholics and 'old-school' diplomats. Britain was to have control of an area roughly comprising Jordan and most of Iraq, plus Haifa in Palestine to allow access to the Mediterranean. France got south-eastern Turkey, northern Iraq, Syria and Lebanon. The two powers were left free to decide state frontiers within these areas. The future of Palestine was to be decided later by an international commission.

The agreement was made public after a copy was discovered in the Russian foreign ministry following the Russian revolution in 1917. By then French and British objectives had changed, and the agreement appeared to contradict both earlier promises made to the Arabs and Britain's new pro-Zionist stance. Its publication caused huge embarrassment to Britain and France.

3 The Balfour Declaration

November 2nd, 1917

Dear Lord Rothschild,

I have much pleasure in conveying to you, on behalf of His Majesty's Government, the following declaration of sympathy with Jewish Zionist aspirations which has been submitted to, and approved by, the Cabinet.

"His Majesty's Government view with favour the establishment in Palestine of a national home for the Jewish people, and will use their best endeavours to facilitate the achievement of this object, it being clearly understood that nothing shall be done which may prejudice the civil and religious rights of existing non-Jewish communities in Palestine, or the rights and political status enjoyed by Jews in any other country."

I should be grateful if you would bring this declaration to the knowledge of the Zionist Federation.

Yours sincerely,

Arthur James Balfour

(For more on Israel and Palestine see Israel and her angry neighbours UGI #147)

4 The King-Crane Commission

Prsident Wilson wanted "men with no previous contact with Syria [to] convince the world that the conference had tried to do all it could to find the most scientific basis possible for a settlement". His commission was led by Henry Churchill King, president of Oberlin College, and Charles Richard Crane, a Chicago businessman and trustee of Robert College in Constantinople. It included a small team of local experts and a translator.

They recommended that: "Whatever foreign administration is brought into Syria should come in, not as a colonising power in the old sense of the term, but as a mandatory under the League of Nations". It should develop a "sacred trust" with the people. The mandate would have a limited term, foster a "national spirit" and set up "institutions of a democratic state" that would guarantee religious liberty while exercising "jealous care over the minorities". The mandated authority should "not take advantage of its position to force a monopolistic control at any point".

The commission recommended "that the unity of Syria be preserved in accordance with the earnest petition of the people of Syria" and that Emir Faisal (see next note) be appointed king. Their principal recommendation for Syria "applies point by point to Mesopotamia". A key recommendation called for a "serious modification of the extreme Zionist program for Palestine", with severe limits on Jewish immigration. Finally, the US, rather than Britain or France, should be the mandatory authority "as the first choice of the people".

The commission met many delegations and considered hundreds of petitions from across the ethnic, religious and political spectrum. Though hardly democratic, it did provide the first opportunity to date for the people of the region to express their views and aspirations. But while King's objectivity was never in doubt, Crane, arguably the more influential of the two, was a known anti-Zionist, making his conclusions suspect to Britain, France and even Wilson himself.

5 Britain and the Arabs

During the late 19th century Britain had encouraged embryonic nationalist movements across the Ottoman empire, hoping an Arab revolt would help it defeat the Ottoman armies. In 1915 the British governor of Egypt in a letter to Sharif Hussein, the ruler of Mecca, promised that Ottoman rule in (Greater) Syria would be replaced by a new Arab state headed by an Arab king. Despite unresolved disputes over frontiers, especially the status pf Palestine, the promise of independence helped to bring over traditional Arab rulers, and an emerging Arab urban middle class to the British side.

But while Sharif Hussein raised an army to fight the Ottomans, British and French officials made the Sykes-Picot Agreement, which on any interpretation is incompatible with the McMahon-Hussein letter. Access to oil was already a significant factor; British control of the oil fields in Persia (now Iran) played an important part in the defeat of Germany.

6 France in Syria and Lebanon

At the end of World War I, Syria, which then included Lebanon, came under French control. French forces ejected Emir Faisal and his Arab government from Damascus in 1919, stoking up nationalist agitation that culminated in an open insurrection in 1925-26. In an attempt to contain ongoing protests, the French authorities played off Syria's and Lebanon's many religious sects against each other. While they did overcome these early waves of popular rebellion, the French methods only strengthened the resentment and determination of the Arabs. Both countries suffered a poisonous rise of sectarianism that would eventually lead to civil war in Lebanon in 1958 and again from 1975 to 1990.

In Lebanon, the Maronite Christians, long regarded as loyal to France, were the greatest beneficiaries of the new order, winning control over the presidency and the army. However, in return for policing their own communities, all religious communities were granted access to the corridors of colonial power. The system developed into a confessional democracy, with all the religious groups competing with each other for power and influence.

7 Wahhabism

In the 1740s in the Arabian peninsula Sheikh Muhammad ibn Wahhab (1703-91) began to preach against the religious and material corruption of the time and to demand a return to the founding principles of Islam, and the simple lifestyle of the 'noble ancestors', the *Salaf*. Central to Ibn Wahhab's message was the doctrine of *Tawhid*, oneness with Allah. Union with God cannot be accomplished through mysticism or rationalism, but through the strict acceptance of the teachings of the Koran. An enduring alliance with the house of Saud enabled the latter to conquer the whole of what is now Saudi Arabia and made Wahhabism the official religion there. Its strict 'purity' seems not to appeal to other Muslims, except perhaps to sections of the Sunni insurgents in Iraq.